LIFE SCIENCE PROJECTS
★ for Kids ★

A PROJECT GUIDE TO

SPONGES, WORMS, AND MOLLUSKS

Colleen Kessler

Mitchell Lane
PUBLISHERS

P.O. Box 196
Hockessin, Delaware 19707
Visit us on the web: www.mitchelllane.com
Comments? email us: mitchelllane@mitchelllane.com

Mitchell Lane
PUBLISHERS

LIFE SCIENCE PROJECTS for Kids

A Project Guide to:
Exploring Earth's Biomes • Fish and Amphibians
Mammals • Projects in Genetics • Reptiles and Birds
Sponges, Worms, and Mollusks

Copyright © 2011 by Mitchell Lane Publishers

All rights reserved. No part of this book may be reproduced without written permission from the publisher. Printed and bound in the United States of America.

PUBLISHER'S NOTE: The facts on which the story in this book is based have been thoroughly researched. Documentation of such research can be found on page 43. While every possible effort has been made to ensure accuracy, the publisher will not assume liability for damages caused by inaccuracies in the data, and makes no warranty on the accuracy of the information contained herein.

Library of Congress
Cataloging-in-Publication Data

Kessler, Colleen.
  A project guide to sponges, worms, and mollusks / Colleen D. Kessler.
     p. cm. — (Life science projects for kids)
  Includes bibliographical references and index.
  ISBN 978-1-58415-876-9 (library bound)
  1. Sponges—Experiments—Juvenile literature. 2. Worms—Experiments—Juvenile literature. 3. Mollusks—Experiments—Juvenile literature. I. Title.
  QL371.6.K47 2011
  593.4078—dc22

2010030944

Printing   1   2   3   4   5   6   7   8   9
                                        PLB

CONTENTS

Introduction...4

Living Filters 10

Diffusing Waste 12

Soak It Up 14

Lean on Me 16

Looking at Leeches 18

Light Sight 22

Many Hearts..24

Totally Tubular...28

Fibonacci Shells..30

Colorful Cuttlefish 34

Slime Time 36

Brain Games 38

Further Reading 42

    Books 42

    On the Internet.................................42

    Works Consulted..............................43

    Science Supply Companies 44

Glossary...45

Index...47

INTRODUCTION

Sponges, worms, and mollusks are simple animals. All simple animals are invertebrates. Some simple animals, like the snail, are able to move from place to place. Others, like the tubeworm, are permanently anchored to the seafloor or another object. An invertebrate does not have a spine made up of bones. Simple animals live in or near water. Most live in the sea, but some can be found on rocks or in ponds, rivers, sand, or mud.

Some simple animals, such as sponges, are filter feeders. This means that they eat tiny pieces of food that float in the water as it flows through their bodies. Others, including worms, are decomposers. Decomposers break down dead plant and animal matter. Worms do this by sucking in their food through their powerful mouths. It passes through the body to their gizzard, where it is ground up and turned into a nutrient-rich waste called a casting. Worm castings are so good for the soil that farmers and gardeners compost with worms. This is called vermicomposting. In exchange for a never-ending food supply, the worms eat and eat, giving their owners buckets of fertilizer.

The simplest of these simple animals is the sponge. Sponges have many cells, but they do not have tissues. Tissues are groups of cells that work together to do the same job—such as heart tissue for pumping blood. When people think about sponges, they often picture the dried,

Yellow tube sponge

colorless natural sponge that many people use in the bathtub. In reality, living sponges come in all shapes and colors. Some can grow to be over 6 feet (2 meters) tall!

Sponges belong to the group Porifera. *Porifera* means "pore bearer." A sponge's body is covered with open pores. Sponges pull water in through their pores, filter the food out of the water, and then eject the water back into the sea. Individual cells digest the trapped food.

There are about 5,000 species of sponges known in the world. Most of these are found in marine waters, but some are found in freshwater. All share similarities. One end is attached to something solid like a rock. The other end is open. Some sponges release toxins to protect themselves against predators. Because of this, other aquatic animals use sponges to protect themselves. Some place adult sponges on their bodies. The sponge attaches itself to a snail shell and encrusts the outer surface of the shell. Some sea snails have been found with their shells completely covered by sponges.

Sea snails belong to another family of simple animals called mollusks. This group includes clams, snails, squid, oysters, scallops, and more. Mollusks are best known for their shells. Some, like the octopus, don't have shells. All mollusks have a mantle of soft skin and a muscular foot that they use for locomotion. Of those that have shells, some, like the

The golden nudibranch, a mollusk, has no shell.

snail, are univalves. This means that they have only one shell. Others, such as clams, are bivalves. They have two shells.

Mollusks are some of the most diverse creatures on Earth. There are as many as 150,000 species, from sea slugs to garden snails, clams to cuttlefish. Some can be very large, like the giant clam, which can reach widths of 4 feet (1.2 meters), or the giant squid, which can be longer than a school bus! Some are tiny. The Pythina clam is only about the size of a single grain of rice.

Giant clam

Just as there is an incredible diversity in the way they look, mollusks consume their food in very different ways. Most bivalves are suspension feeders. They pull their food from water that they suck into their bodies, then eject the water back out when they've finished. Some use a radula, a structure that has many tiny sharp teeth, to scrape algae off rocks and other objects. Still others, like snails, are scavengers. They use a radula to eat decaying plant and animal matter from the bottom of ponds and rivers.

One of the most well known scavengers, the earthworm, is another simple animal. The earthworm belongs to the annelid, or segmented worm, group. There are several other groups that make up the worm family. There are flatworms, ribbon worms, roundworms, and more. Worms usually have a long, tubelike body with no arms or legs. They can vary in length from less than a half inch (1 centimeter) to over 100 feet (30 meters) long.

Some worms are parasites. A parasite is an animal that lives on or in another organism like a plant or animal—even a human! The pinworm is a type of parasitic roundworm that can infect humans. It lives and lays eggs in and around its host's anus, causing severe itching. Another parasitic worm that can infect humans is the Guinea worm. This worm infects humans, mostly in Africa, when they drink water that contains microscopic water fleas. The fleas carry even tinier Guinea worm larvae. The worms pierce their host's intestinal walls as they mature, grow, and mate. The male worms die, and the females continue to make their way to their host's skin, growing as they travel. They can grow to be as large as three feet (one meter) long! They settle in their human host's legs, causing painful burning and blistering. Gross!

Worms are as diverse a group as the sponges and mollusks. There are hundreds of thousands of types. From earthworms to leeches, tapeworms to spaghetti worms, they can be found in just about every ecological habitat on Earth.

Birds and many other animals prey on worms.

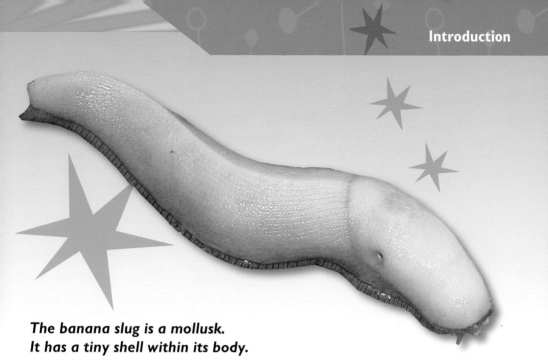

The banana slug is a mollusk.
It has a tiny shell within its body.

Throughout history, scientists, ecologists, and nature lovers have been fascinated by the diversity of sponges, worms, and mollusks. These animals can be found just about anywhere, and they come in many sizes, shapes, and forms. In this book, you will learn about these animals, along with some of their habits, preferences, and defining characteristics. Some of the hands-on activities presented here are perfect to try at home; others can be adapted or used for science fairs and school projects. All of them are fun and will help you learn something about the animals that make up your world.

When you try these activities, keep track of your results and observations in a notebook. Successful scientists record their observations from the field. They do this by keeping a field journal. When scientists record what they see and do, others can learn from the scientists' experiences and build on their knowledge. A science note-book can work the same way for you. You'll be able to look back and see what you've done, and build on your own learning. You'll also have a record of the science you've done just for fun! Use your science notebook with each of the activities in this book—a plain spiral notebook will do the job.

Remember to respect the animals you are studying—whether you are out in their natural habitat or they are pets in yours. Be kind and gentle, and treat them carefully. Most of all, have fun being a scientist!

LIVING FILTERS

A sponge is a sessile organism. This means that it can't move from one place to another on its own. Can you imagine what it would be like to have your feet permanently attached to the ground? You would not be able to go to the kitchen to get your own food. Sponges can't move to get food, either. They must wait for it to come to them.

A sponge is a filter feeder. It takes its food from the water that flows through it. Using its flagella, long whipping tails, it circulates water through its pores. Tiny particles of food are then filtered out of the water. Then, the sponge pushes the water back out through a hole called the osculum.

Now it's your turn to act like a sponge. Become sessile, and anchor yourself in your kitchen to try this activity.

PROCEDURE
1. Put a handful of salad greens into the blender. Cover them with water and blend them for a few seconds. You want some small pieces of salad to float to the top and some to mix with the water. Do not eliminate all the solid pieces.

MATERIALS

* mixed salad greens
* blender
* water
* coffee filter
* scale or balance
* strainer
* clear container
* science notebook

2. Record your observations about the appearance of the solution.
3. Weigh a dry coffee filter on a scale or balance. Record this weight in your notebook.
4. Place a strainer over a clear container. Place the dry coffee filter inside the strainer.
5. Pour plain water through the coffee filter. Weigh this saturated filter and record its weight in your notebook. This represents a sponge that is in the water, as it would always be saturated.
6. Dump the water out of the clear container and put the strainer with the wet filter back on top.
7. Carefully, pour the blended solution through the coffee filter. Observe the solution that makes it into the clear container. Record your observations in your notebook. How is this solution different than the solution you poured from the blender?
8. Weigh the coffee filter one more time. This new weight represents the water absorbed by the sponge and the filtered food.
9. How much food was trapped by the filter? You can find this out by subtracting the weight of the wet filter from the weight of the wet filter with food. This number represents the food your "sponge" has trapped inside its body.

DIFFUSING WASTE

Sponges pump an incredible amount of water through their bodies every day. Water containing food goes in, and water containing waste goes out. The food that enters a sponge's body is transferred to its cells. Then, like all animals, simple or not, the sponge creates waste products that need to be eliminated.

The release of a sponge's waste is one example of how ocean life is interconnected. Sponges release waste products—such as carbon dioxide, nitrogen, and ammonia—into the water through a process called diffusion. When something is diffused, it is spread out. Scientists believe that the nitrogen diffused by sponges helps fertilize seaweed and other marine plants. In this activity, you will see how a substance can move through water by diffusion.

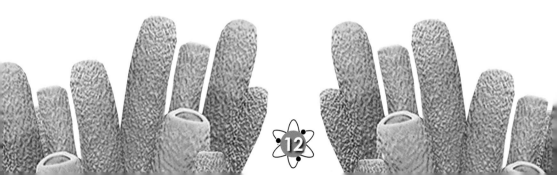

MATERIALS
* shallow pan of water
* flat surface
* food coloring
* electric fan
* **an adult**

PROCEDURE
1. Place a pan of water on a table or other flat surface.
2. Put a few drops of food coloring in the water near one end of the pan.
3. Turn an electric fan on low and have **an adult** direct the air right onto the surface of the water where the food coloring is.
4. The color should spread slowly through the water, mixing with it. This is how the waste gases move through the water when they are released by a sponge.

SOAK IT UP

Humans have used sponges for centuries. As far back as the time of ancient Greek philosopher Plato (c. 428–348 BCE), sponges have been used for bathing. They were also used as portable drinking devices, as padding for battle helmets, and to filter drinking water. New uses for sponges are constantly being discovered as humans continue to harvest these incredible invertebrates as tools.

Scientists have observed dolphins taking advantage of sea sponges to help them solve problems, too. Female dolphins in Western Australia's Shark Bay attach a sponge to their beak, and then nose around the ocean floor in search of food. Scientists suspect that the sponges protect the dolphins from the stinging stonefish that hide on the ocean floor.

Sponges are helpful tools—to both humans and dolphins—because of their porosity. Porosity is the property of being porous, or having holes (pores) that absorb liquids. It can be measured by comparing the volume of air in a sponge to its total volume. In this activity, you can find out just how much air space, or how porous, a sponge is.

MATERIALS

* natural sponge (available at grocery stores)
* faucet
* clear measuring cylinder

PROCEDURE

1. Hold a natural sponge under running water.
2. Repeatedly squeeze it and let go until you have forced out all of the air and the sponge is full of water.
3. As quickly as you can, move the saturated sponge to the measuring cylinder and squeeze out all of the water. Keep squeezing until you have gotten as much of the water as possible into the cylinder.
4. Look at the markings on the cylinder to measure the water. This will be the approximate volume of the sponge's air space—its porosity.

LEAN ON ME

Animals have many amazing adaptations that help them survive in their environments. Even sessile sponges have found some unique ways to make up for their lack of movement. Sponges have been known to form special relationships with other marine animals. For example, some sponges attach themselves to hermit crab shells. When the hermit crab walks across the ocean floor, it takes the sponge with it. In exchange for a ride, the sponge protects the hermit crab from predators. This type of relationship, in which both parties benefit, is called symbiosis.

Some sponges have a symbiotic relationship with algae. Algae are simple plants that sometimes live within a sponge's body. The algae provide oxygen and food for the sponge, while the sponge provides the algae with carbon dioxide and a safe home.

In this activity, you will get a sense of what it might be like for a sponge that relies on another animal to move it from place to place.

MATERIALS
* blindfold
* a friend

PROCEDURE

1. Decide which of you will be the hermit crab and which will be the sponge. Blindfold the "sponge."
2. The "hermit crab" should guide the sponge around the house or yard. The crab might stop from time to time to sleep, move slowly, move quickly away from predators, or jab at prey with jerky motions.
3. Have the "sponge" take the blindfold off and talk about what it was like not being able to decide where he or she was going. Have the "hermit crab" talk about what it was like to bring another animal everywhere he or she went.
4. Switch roles.
5. For added fun, create an obstacle course for the hermit crab to navigate.

LOOKING AT LEECHES

Leeches are brownish black segmented worms that have suckers on each of their ends. They can range in size from an inch (2.5 centimeters) to more than 10 inches (25 centimeters). Some of them feed on dead or decaying plant and animal matter. Others are parasites that feed on the blood of living animals.

Parasitic leeches can feed on blood in one of two ways. Some puncture the skin of an animal—or human—with a long snout called a proboscis. Others use their three jaws and tiny razor-sharp teeth to chomp at their host. A leech's saliva contains a chemical that can numb its prey's body, prevent clotting, and prevent infection. Because the host's blood doesn't clot, but continues to flow, leeches can continue to drink until they are dislodged from the animal's body. They consume a lot of blood this way, taking advantage of being on the host animal, so they don't have to feed often.

Throughout history, doctors have used leeches to remove "excess" blood from a person's body. People in the past believed that this practice restored the human body's balance. Imagine being the person employed to collect leeches for medical purposes. Since leeches are

* leech—commonly sold as bait at tackle stores or through online bait and tackle retailers
DO NOT ATTEMPT TO HARVEST POND LEECHES YOURSELF!
* Petri dish ¾ full of water
* garden gloves (or other canvas gloves) or nonmetal tongs
* bright lamp
* 2 small glass dishes or beakers
* beef broth
* vinegar
* 2 eyedroppers
* water

able to detect an animal's skin, oils, and blood, you would wade into a leech-infested pond and wait for the leeches to find you. After dozens of them attached to your legs and you walked back to shore, a handler would remove them from your body and sell them to a doctor. Ouch!

In this activity, you will observe leeches to see how they find their food. Be careful when you are handling the leech. Do this experiment only with the help of **an adult.** Do not touch the leech directly or harm it in any way.

PROCEDURE

1. Wearing gloves or using nonmetal tongs, gently place a leech in a Petri dish of water.
2. Observe the leech's behavior. What is it doing? How does it move? Record your observations in your science notebook.
3. Place the Petri dish under a bright lamp. How does the leech react to the light? Cast a shadow by placing your hand between the lamp and the Petri dish. How does the leech react? Record your observations.
4. Place the leech in a clean beaker with a little clean water. Using an eyedropper, place beef broth in the beaker, one drop at a time.

Count how many drops it takes before the leech reacts. What does it do? Why do you think it does this? Record your observations.

5. Place the leech back into its original Petri dish for a few minutes to allow it to rest.

6. Next, place the leech in a clean beaker with water. Using a new eyedropper, add vinegar one drop at a time until the leech reacts. (Be careful to drop the vinegar in the water, not directly on the leech.) How many drops does it take before the leech reacts? What does it do? Why do you think this is? Record your observations, and then return the leech to the Petri dish.

Look at your recordings. How was the leech affected by light? By odor? What can this information tell you about its habits?

When you are finished with this activity, you can set up a mini habitat for your leech and observe it for some time. All you need is a clear container, clean water, and a piece of gauze secured to the top of the container to let air through but keep the leech in. Since leeches tend to gorge themselves when they eat, they can go long periods of time between feedings. In the wild, one large feeding can keep a leech alive for an entire season! When feeding your new pet, though, you'll want to offer food a little more often than once a year. Place a small piece of fresh liver from the grocery store into the water once a month. Let your leech feed overnight, remove the liver, and replace the water in the container with fresh.

LIGHT SIGHT

Imagine being blinded by a glowing, green light coming at you from the depths of the sea. What could it be? It's a . . . a . . . worm? That's just what happened to Karen Osborn of Scripps Institution of Oceanography at the University of California, San Diego. She and some of her colleagues explored ocean depths between 5,900 and 12,140 feet (1,800 and 3,700 meters) with remote-controlled vehicles.

Her group discovered seven new species of worms, five of which are bioluminescent. *Bioluminescence* means "living light"; bioluminescent animals and plants can produce a glow. Animals in the sea use bioluminescence as a means of protection, as well as a way to attract prey. Some animals use it as a way to communicate with other animals of the same species.

Osborn's new "glowworm" is a bit different, though. She and the other scientists on her team have nicknamed them "green bombers" because they release body parts to create a green "bomb" that lights up as it is released. The bombs glow vividly for a few seconds and then fade away.

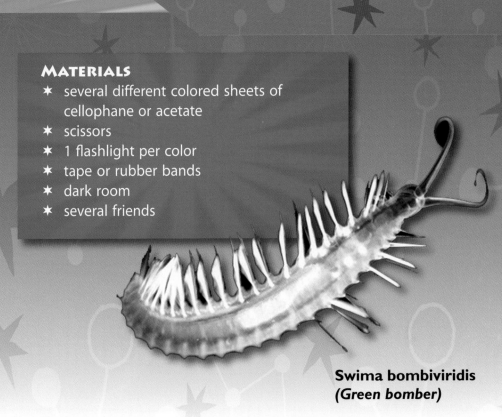

MATERIALS

* several different colored sheets of cellophane or acetate
* scissors
* 1 flashlight per color
* tape or rubber bands
* dark room
* several friends

**Swima bombiviridis
(Green bomber)**

Scientists can only speculate what these bombs are for. Do they frighten predators? Attract prey? Or communicate with similar animals? In this activity, you will play with "bioluminescence" as a means of communicating with friends.

PROCEDURE

1. Cut a square of each color of cellophane or acetate large enough to cover the light on each flashlight. Secure the cellophane or acetate to the flashlights with tape or rubber bands. Give each person a flashlight.
2. In a dark room, experiment with different colors. Flash your lights on and off toward each other. Can you see some colors better than others? Which ones? Why do you think this is?
3. Try leaving the light on for long and short flashes. Is a long flash easier or more difficult to see than a short flash? Why? What happens when your friends move their lights while they are on?
4. Try to create a "language" for communicating with your lights. A series of short flashes followed by a long flash could mean "Let's go for a snack." A rapid flash, flash, flash could mean, "Okay!"

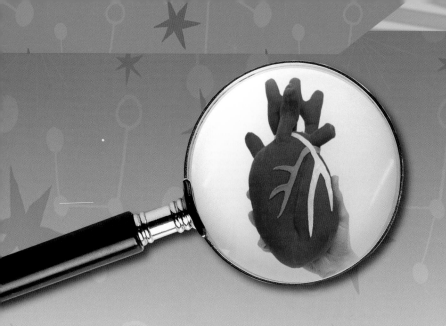

MANY HEARTS

A human's heart beats about 70 times each minute. With each beat, blood is pushed throughout the body, bringing oxygen and other nutrients to the cells.

Imagine if you had five separate hearts beating rapidly together in your body. How quickly could your blood travel then? Earthworms have five hearts located in their anterior section. Together, these five hearts move blood to all areas of the worm's body. Most earthworms grow to be about 12 inches (30 centimeters) long. The longest earthworm ever discovered was found in South Africa. It was almost 264 inches (6.7 meters) long! That worm's hearts had to push its blood a long way!

Humans breathe using lungs. Oxygen and carbon dioxide are exchanged with each breath. Although earthworms have many hearts, they do not have lungs. They breathe through their skin. Their bodies must stay moist for them to be able to breathe.

In this activity, you can see a worm's hearts at work. Watch carefully—they beat fast! If you have trouble obtaining a worm, you can use a computer with Internet access to check out a video of an earthworm's hearts beating (such as the one at All About Earthworms: http://yucky. discovery.com/flash/worm/pg000102.html; click on Heartbeat Video).

* earthworm (easy to find under rocks, in garden soil, and on the pavement after it rains, or you can get them from a bait shop)
* paper towels
* spray bottle filled with water
* Petri or other clear dish
* microscope or strong magnifying glass
* watch or clock with second hand OR a timer

Like humans and other vertebrates, earthworms have blood vessels for delivering nutrients to the body. Mollusks and most other invertebrates, however, do not have blood vessels. Their blood is pumped directly into body cavities.

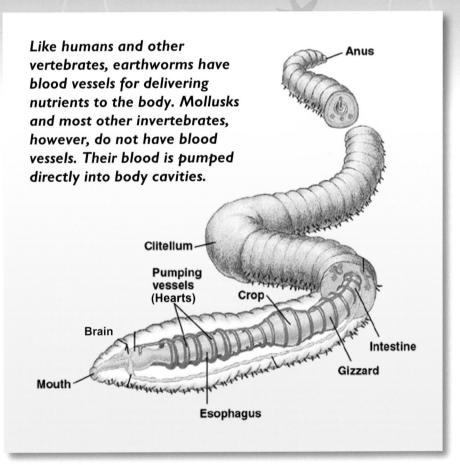

PROCEDURE

1. Take your pulse by placing two fingers (not your thumb) at your wrist and counting the beats for one minute. Record your pulse.
2. Place your earthworm on a moist paper towel or, if you are using a microscope, in a clear dish that has been spritzed with water.
3. To observe your earthworm's heartbeats, find the clitellum, or saddle area. The anterior section is the shorter end of the body. An earthworm's hearts lie very close together about halfway between the mouth tip and the saddle.
4. For a clearer view of the heartbeats, place the clear dish on the microscope stage. If you do not have a microscope, look closely through a magnifying glass and locate the hearts. Notice that the hearts seem to "ripple" as they beat. Each ripple is made up of the five hearts beating one after another, one time. This ripple counts as one heartbeat. Make sure to spritz your worm with water if it gets dry.
5. Have a friend time you for one minute as you count your worm's heartbeats. If you are doing this activity yourself, set a timer for one minute and count until the timer goes off. This is your worm's pulse.
6. Figure out how many times the earthworm's hearts beat for every one of your heartbeats by dividing the worm's pulse by your pulse.
7. Let's do some math to figure out whether your heart or the worm's hearts will beat more over the course of a lifetime. On average, healthy humans live for approximately 78 years. Multiply the following:
   a. Your pulse (heartbeats per minute) x 60 minutes = Heartbeats per hour
   b. Heartbeats per hour x 24 hours = Heartbeats per day
   c. Heartbeats per day x 365 days = Heartbeats per year
   d. Heartbeats per year x 78 years = Heartbeats per lifetime
8. An earthworm can live for about 10 years if it avoids becoming another animal's prey. Try this formula to determine how many times your earthworm's heart will beat over its lifetime:
   a. Earthworm's pulse (heartbeats per minute) x 60 minutes = Earthworm's heartbeats per hour

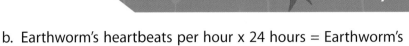
b. Earthworm's heartbeats per hour x 24 hours = Earthworm's heartbeats per day

c. Earthworm's heartbeats per day x 365 days = Earthworm's heartbeats per year

d. Earthworm's heartbeats per year x 10 years = Earthworm's heartbeats per lifetime

9. Which one—you or the earthworm—will have more heartbeats over the course of a lifetime?

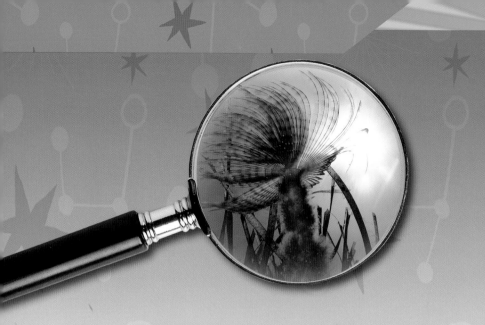

TOTALLY TUBULAR

A mile and a half (2.4 kilometers) below the surface of the Pacific Ocean lies an unusual sight. A community of animals thrives around hydrothermal vents in the ocean floor. A hydrothermal vent is a superheated spring flowing from a crack at the bottom of the ocean. Surrounding these vents are some of the strangest looking creatures on Earth. Among these is the tubeworm. Tubeworms grow in clusters of up to a million animals. Each one shares a symbiotic relationship with a special type of bacteria.

The bacteria live inside the tubeworm's body, giving the worm a constant source of nourishment. Because their food source lives inside them, tubeworms don't have a mouth or digestive system. They simply absorb energy from their food directly into their cells.

Tubeworms all have mouths and guts when they are born. Adults release their eggs into the water, where they are fertilized. When the larvae hatch, they swim down to the ocean floor near the vent, anchor themselves permanently, and swallow bacteria. As they grow, their mouths and guts disappear, trapping the bacteria inside. Tubeworms have long, red tentacles that extend into the ocean. They look like large

MATERIALS

* paper plate with a hole punched through the middle
* marshmallow
* white chocolate candy melts
* microwave
* microwave-safe dish
* thick red licorice, cut to about 5 inches long

lipstick tubes up to eight feet (2.4 meters) tall. When a tubeworm senses danger, it retreats into its tube for safety. Try making your own model of a tubeworm in this activity.

PROCEDURE

1. Place a paper plate on the table. This represents the ocean floor.
2. Put a handful of white chocolate melts in a microwave-safe dish and place it in the microwave. Melt the chocolate, stopping to stir every few seconds. NOTE: Chocolate that is made for melting—sold in craft and food stores for making candy—does not need to get super hot in order to melt. It also hardens quickly, so take care not to overheat it, and use it right away once it is melted.
3. Roll a marshmallow in the chocolate and stand it up on the ocean floor (paper plate) directly over the hole. Give it some time to harden, or put it in the refrigerator for five minutes to speed up the process. This is the tube in which your tubeworm will live.
4. Insert the licorice into the top of the marshmallow, and pull it through the hole in the plate. This is its tentacle. Pull on the licorice carefully, making the worm pull its tentacle into its tube.
5. If you want, you can repeat this activity several times, using the same paper plate with additional holes punched in it. You'll end up with a colony of edible tubeworms.
6. Once you've admired your model, enjoy your snack!

FIBONACCI SHELLS

Have you ever collected Fibonacci patterns? If you've ever gathered seashells at the beach, you've had your hands on Fibonacci numbers.

Fibonacci, also known as Leonardo of Pisa, was a mathematician who lived during the Middle Ages. He was born in Italy and educated in North Africa. He loved to explore numbers and their relationships—especially for these numbers:

1, 1, 2, 3, 5, 8, 13, 21, 34, 55 . . .

Do you see a pattern?

Look at the first two numbers (1, 1). Add them together. What do you get? (2) Now add that number to the one before it (1). You get the next number, 3. Add that number to the next number (5). What do you get? (8) Keep adding numbers in this pattern: 5 + 8 = 13; 8 + 13 = 21.

The Fibonacci pattern is seen in many places in nature. Most flowers follow it, whether it is the spiraling petal pattern of a rose or the seeds in a sunflower head. Pineapples, pinecones, and seashells all follow the pattern, too.

*Fibonacci patterns
in nature*

Seashells are hard structures that protect the soft, spineless bodies within them. Some of the mollusks that produce shells in a spiral pattern are the conch, nautilus, and snail.

PROCEDURE

1. In the center of a sheet of graph paper, draw a square, one unit by one unit. This represents the first 1 in the Fibonacci sequence.

2. Draw a second square next to the first square. This represents the second 1 in the sequence.

3. Draw a third square that is 2 units by 2 units on top of the first two squares. This area represents the 2 in the Fibonacci sequence.

4. Draw a fourth square that is 3 units by 3 units to the left of the first three squares. This represents the 3 in the Fibonacci sequence. If you add the length of the sides of the squares touching the new square, you'll see that you have 1 unit plus 2 units touching 3 units (1 + 2 = 3).

5. Draw a fifth square that is 5 units by 5 units below the first four squares. This represents the 5 in the Fibonacci sequence. If you add the length of the sides of the squares touching the new square, you'll see that you have 3 units plus 1 unit plus 1 unit touching 5 units (3 + 1 + 1 = 5).

6. Draw a sixth square that is 8 units by 8 units to the right of the first five squares.

7. Continue to add squares to your diagram until you fill the page. You can attach more pages to the first piece of graph paper if you want to make it really large.

8. Connect opposite corners of each square with quarter circles, starting with the first square you drew. See the photograph on page 30 for what this should look like.

9. Compare your drawing with the seashell or photograph you used as a reference. Do you see the similarities?

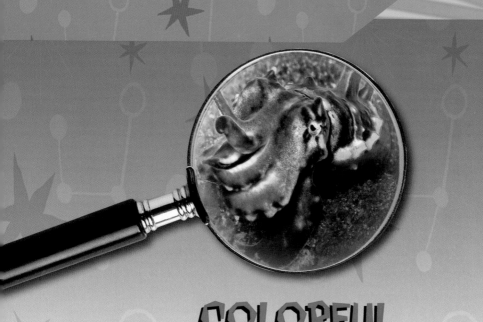

COLORFUL CUTTLEFISH

Cuttlefish are very intelligent mollusks that live in the sea. They are sometimes called "chameleons of the sea" because they have the ability to change their appearance. Actually, though, their color-changing abilities are vastly superior to those of the chameleon. Not only can they change their color, but they can also change the texture of their skin! They have bands of muscle that contract and bulge. Liquid in the center of their muscles gets forced up, forming points, spikes, nodes, or flat blades. This ability, coupled with their color changes, allows them to take on the appearance of rocks, sponges, seaweed, and other sea objects.

Not only do cuttlefish use this adaptation for camouflage, but scientists believe that changing their pattern is one way that cuttlefish communicate. They can flash and ripple patterns as they try to impress a mate. Scientists believe that cuttlefish even use their patterning and flashing to hypnotize prey.

They also believe cuttlefish are colorblind. So how do they change colors to match their environment? Cuttlefish have over 200 specialized pigment cells called chromatophores per 0.001 square inch (1 square millimeter) of their skin. Each pigment cell contains black, brown, red,

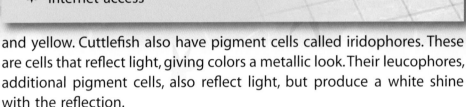

* graph paper, preferably ¼ inch x ¼ inch (you can make your own graph paper here: http://incompetech.com/graphpaper/plain/)
* colored pencils: black, brown, red, and yellow
* Internet access

and yellow. Cuttlefish also have pigment cells called iridophores. These are cells that reflect light, giving colors a metallic look. Their leucophores, additional pigment cells, also reflect light, but produce a white shine with the reflection.

Cuttlefish do most of their color matching in a passive way. Their leucophores reflect the light, sending a signal to the cuttlefish's brain. Then the brain signals the chromatophores, which have bands of muscle radiating from their center, like the spokes on a wheel. These muscles contract and relax to expose or hide different hues of color. This entire communication takes place in less time than it takes you to blink your eye.

PROCEDURE

1. Using only your graph paper and the four cuttlefish colors, create different patterns to communicate different ideas. For example, your patterns might say:

   "Come here."
   "Stay away."
   "I'm hungry."
   "I'm tired."
   "Let's play."

   Why did you select each particular pattern?
2. Create a pattern that might hypnotize your prey. Why do you think this pattern might distract your dinner?
3. Compare your patterns to some Internet images of cuttlefish. You can find images at sites such as *NOVA: Kings of Camouflage* (http://www.pbs.org/wgbh/nova/camo/change.html) and *A to Z Animals: Cuttlefish* (http://a-z-animals.com/animals/cuttlefish/). How do your patterns compare with what a cuttlefish can do in nature?

SLIME TIME

Snails are some of the most common mollusks. In fact, they are almost as widely distributed as insects! They can be found in just about any habitat, from deserts to wetlands, mountains to forests, ponds to the depths of the ocean. The largest, the giant Ghana snail of Africa, can grow to be as long as 12 inches (30 centimeters) and weigh up to 2 pounds (nearly 1 kilogram)!

A snail's body is basically a head with a long flat foot. In fact, *gastropod,* the name for the class to which snails and slugs belong, means "stomach-foot." Snails are gastropods that grow a spiral-shaped shell for protection from their many predators.

They just might be best known for the slime trail they leave behind, though. Snail slime is made up of mostly mucus and water. It acts as both a glue and a lubricant (grease) that helps snails get around. A snail creeps along on its long flat foot as it secretes its slime. The slime allows the snail to grip and climb smooth surfaces, even if they are completely vertical. The slime "glues" them to the surface, and as they push themselves forward, the slime lets go and then acts as a lubricant so that they can move smoothly. A snail is actually sticking to and gliding along a surface at the same time with different parts of its body. A band of muscles in the foot contracts and expands, creating a rippling motion that propels the snail forward.

You can watch how a snail gets around in this locomotion activity.

MATERIALS

* several garden snails from your backyard, nearby woods, or park
* rigid sheet of clear plastic or acrylic, or clear plastic aquarium with water
* bricks, books, or something else to prop one side of the sheet of plastic

PROCEDURE

1. Prop one end of the sheet of clear plastic on bricks or books. Make sure it is slanted enough for you to see under it. Place one snail on the plastic, near the middle. A snail in a clear plastic aquarium will also work well.
2. Once the snail begins to move, watch it from underneath. (This may take a while, so be patient!)
3. The foot grips the plastic while the rippling muscles move it forward. Do you see the slime secretion?
4. Line up several snails. Draw their positions in your science notebook, then draw their new positions every few minutes. Does their movement seem random? Or does it seem to have a pattern?

Be sure to return your snails to the exact location you found them, give them to a teacher to keep as a class pet, or keep them yourself. If you want to keep them as a pet, prepare a clean terrarium with moss or compost on the bottom, safe places to hide (perhaps plastic or terra-cotta pots), and fresh fruits and vegetables. Keep the moss or compost damp.

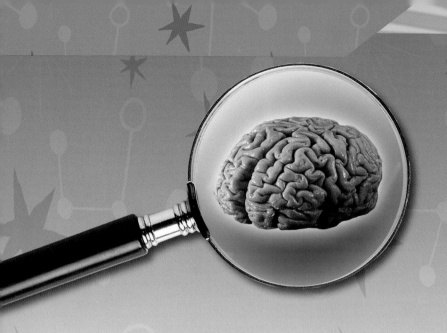

BRAIN GAMES

One of the most intelligent sea mollusks is the octopus. This cephalopod ("head-foot") can shorten, elongate, twist, and bend its many arms to catch prey, build shelter, and even open jars! An octopus can problem solve to get its food. Clam shells are difficult to open, but an octopus will try several different methods to open one. First it will try to flip it open. If that doesn't work, it may try to pry it open using a rock, or it will drill into it using its radula. Usually an octopus will try several methods before giving up.

Octopus movement has fascinated scientists for some time. These animals move by crawling and creeping along the rocky bottom of the sea with their arms and suckers. When they are scared, though, they shoot backward by ejecting a stream of water through a siphon. They can also squirt an inky substance to screen their escape.

Scientists have discovered that an octopus's arms are arranged as four sets, with two limbs each. Movement is guided separately by each set of limbs, not just by the brain. This means that the brain "tells" the arms where it wants to go, and the arms "decide" for themselves how to get there.

MATERIALS
* you and four friends
* video recorder (optional)

In this activity, you get to be an octopus "brain" and direct your "limbs" by shouting information to your friends.

PROCEDURE

1. Decide who will be the brain of the octopus. Give the brain the video recorder if you are planning to use one.

Four people lock arms and try to move like an octopus.

2. Have the remaining four friends sit in a circle on the floor with their backs touching and facing outward.
3. Have the four friends, or limbs, lock arms to form a single octopus. Have the octopus stand up.
4. The brain should give the octopus directions, like, "Walk toward the door." Each "limb" will have to think about how it will get there. For example, one limb (friend) will need to walk forward toward the door, one sideways to the right, one sideways to the left, and one backward.
5. Have the brain give several other simple directions while video recording the limb movements.
6. Watch the video or talk with your friends about the experience. What did you learn about the movement of an octopus during this activity? Was it difficult for all of the limbs to work together?
7. Switch roles so that everyone gets a chance to be the "brain."

Books

Batten, Mary. *The Winking, Blinking Sea: All about Bioluminescence.* Brookfield, CT: The Millbrook Press, 2000.

Blaxland, Beth. *Earthworms, Leeches, and Sea Worms.* Philadelphia: Chelsea House, 2002.

Cassie, Brian. *National Audubon Society First Field Guide: Shells.* New York: Scholastic, 2000.

Gilpin, Daniel. *Snails, Shellfish & Other Mollusks.* Minneapolis, MN: Compass Point, 2006.

Hall, David. *Octopuses and Squids.* Danbury, CT: Children's Press, 2006.

Hirschmann, Kris. *Sponges: Creatures of the Sea.* Farmington Hills, MI: KidHaven Press, 2005.

Parker, Steve. *Nematodes, Leeches, & Other Worms.* Minneapolis, MN: Compass Point, 2006.

———. *Sponges, Jellyfish, & Other Simple Animals.* Minneapolis, MN: Compass Point, 2006.

Petersen, Christine. *Invertebrates.* New York: Franklin Watts, 2002.

On the Internet

BrainPop: Mollusks
>   http://www.brainpop.com/science/diversityoflife/mollusks/preview.weml

Kidipede—History and Science for Middle School Kids:
>   Cephalopods:
>>   http://www.historyforkids.org/scienceforkids/biology/animals/cephalopods/index.htm
>   Mollusks:
>>   http://www.historyforkids.org/scienceforkids/biology/animals/mollusks/
>   Segmented Worms:
>>   http://www.historyforkids.org/scienceforkids/biology/animals/segmentedworms/
>   Sponges:
>>   http://www.historyforkids.org/scienceforkids/biology/animals/sponges/

Sheppard Software—Mollusk Games and Profiles:
>   http://www.sheppardsoftware.com/content/animals/profile_mollusks.htm

The Yuckiest Site on the Internet—Discovery Kids: Earthworms; Leeches
>   http://yucky.discovery.com/flash/worm/pg000102.html
>   http://yucky.discovery.com/flash/worm/pg000219.html

Learning Games for Kids: Octopus Games and Videos
>   http://www.learninggamesforkids.com/animal-games-octopus.html

Works Consulted

"About Sponges." *Tree of Life Web Project.* Accessed August 19, 2010.
http://tolweb.org/treehouses/?treehouse_id=3431

Allen, Catherine Judge. *Corals, Jellyfishes, Sponges, and Other Simple Animals.*
Farmington Hills, MI: Thompson Gale, 2005.

Anderson, Matt, Jeffrey Frazier, and Kris Popendorf. "Leonard Fibonacci."
http://library.thinkquest.org/27890/biographies1.html

"Bacteria From Sponges Make New Pharmaceuticals." *ScienceDaily,* September 7, 2007.
http://www.sciencedaily.com/releases/2007/09/070903204947.htm

Blackburn, Laura. "Agile Animals." *Journal of Experimental Biology* (2005): iv-vi. Accessed
August 20, 2010. http://jeb.biologists.org/cgi/reprint/208/21/v.pdf.

"Coe College Biology Department: Hermit Crab Sponges."
http://www.public.coe.edu/departments/Biology/hermit.html

"Cuttlefish Change Color, Shape-Shift to Elude Predators." *Daily Nature and Science
News and Headlines | National Geographic News,* August 6, 2008. Accessed August
18, 2010. http://news.nationalgeographic.com/news/2008/08/080608-cuttlefish-
camouflage-missions.html

Discovery Channel. The Ultimate Guide: Octopus: Cuttlefish Communications.
http://videos.howstuffworks.com/discovery/29075-the-ultimate-guide-octopus-
cuttlefish-communication-video.htm

El-Awady, Aisha. "Maggots and Leeches Make a Comeback." *Science in Africa,* July–
August 2003. http://www.scienceinafrica.co.za/2003/july/leech.htm

Glenday, Craig (editor). *Guinness World Records 2009.* New York: Bantam Publishing,
2009.

Holloway, Margaret. "Cuttlefish Say It with Skin." *Natural History,* April, 2000.
http://findarticles.com/p/articles/mi_m1134/is_3_109/ai_61524425/
?tag=content;col1

Keim, Brandon. "Acrobatic Octopus Arm Could Be Model for Flexible Robots." *Wired
Science,* September 17, 2009. http://www.wired.com/wiredscience/2009/09/
octopuscontrol/

Lawrence, Leah. "Bloodletting: An Early Treatment Used by Barbers, Surgeons."
Cardiology Today, September 1, 2008. http://www.cardiologytoday.com/view.
aspx?rid=31588

"Mollusks Page 1—Coral Reef Life on Sea and Sky." *Sea and Sky—Explore the Oceans
Below and the Skies Above.* Accessed August 20, 2010. http://www.seasky.org/
reeflife/sea2f.html

Myers, Phil. "ADW: Porifera: Information." *Animal Diversity Web.* Accessed August 19,
2010. http://animaldiversity.ummz.umich.edu/site/accounts/information/
Porifera.html

NOAA: "Filter Feeding in Reef Sponges."
http://oceanservice.noaa.gov/education/yos/lesson/Grades%203-5/filter_feed_sponge_lesson.pdf

"NOVA | Kings of Camouflage | Quick Change Artists." PBS. Accessed August 18, 2010. http://www.pbs.org/wgbh/nova/camo/change.html.

Octopus Project. http://www.octopusproject.eu/

Owens, James. "Dolphin Moms Teach Daughters to Use Tools." *National Geographic,* June 7, 2005. http://news.nationalgeographic.com/news/2005/06/0607_050607_dolphin_tools.html

Scripps Institution of Oceanography. "Scientists Discover Bioluminescent 'Green Bombers' from the Deep Sea." InSciences Organisation, August 20, 2009. http://insciences.org/article.php?article_id=6542

Sea and Sky presents "Creatures of the Deep Sea: Tubeworms." Accessed August 18, 2010. http://www.seasky.org/deep-sea/giant-tube-worm.html

Smolker, R.A., et al. "Sponge-carrying by Indian Ocean Bottlenose Dolphins: Possible Tool-use by a Delphinid." *Ethology* 103: 454–465, 1997.

Stidworthy, John. *Simple Animals.* New York: Facts on File, Inc., 1990.

Vacelet, J. "A New Genus of Carnivorous Sponges (Porifera: Poecilosclerida, Cladorhizidae) from the Deep N-E Pacific, and Remarks on the Genus Neocladia." *Zootaxa* 1752: 57–65; April 15, 2008. http://www.mapress.com/zootaxa/2008/f/z01752p065f.pdf

"The Wonders of the Seas: Mollusks." *Oceanic Research Group.* Accessed August 20, 2010. http://www.oceanicresearch.org/education/wonders/mollusk.html

Wyman, Bruce, Ph.D., and L. Harold Stevenson, Ph.D. *The Facts on File Dictionary of Environmental Science* (Third Edition). New York: Infobase Publishing, 2007.

Science Supply Companies

Carolina Biological Supply—science supplies and live organisms
http://www.carolina.com/home.do

Delta Education—science supplies and live organisms
http://www.delta-education.com

Home Science Tools—science supplies
http://www.hometrainingtools.com/

Steve Spangler Science—science supplies

anus (AY-nus)—The opening at the end of the digestive tract.

anterior (an-TEER-ee-ur)—Near the head or front of the body.

bioluminescence (by-oh-loo-mih-NEH-sents)—The emission of visible light from the body.

casting (KAS-ting)—Undigested materials and soil excreted by worms.

cephalopod (SEH-fuh-loh-pod)—Meaning "head-foot," a mollusk with a large head and tentacles, such as an octopus, squid, or cuttlefish.

chromatophore (kroh-MAA-tuh-for)—Animal cells that contain pigments.

clitellum (klih-TEL-um)—The thickened area on the body of a worm.

compost (KOM-pohst)—A mixture of decaying vegetation and manure used for fertilizer.

decomposer (dee-kum-POH-zer)—An organism that breaks down dead or decaying plant or animal matter.

diffusion (dih-FYOO-zhun)—The property of being dispersed or spread out.

Fibonacci (fih-boh-NAHT-chee) **pattern**—A numerical relationship developed by Fibonacci (Leonardo of Pisa: c.1170 – c.1250), one of the greatest mathematicians of the Middle Ages. In the pattern, the next number is the result of adding the two previous numbers (1, 1, 2, 3, 5, 8, 13, 21, . . .).

filter feeder—An animal that filters tiny pieces of food from a current of water.

flagellum (flah-JEL-um)—A tail-like limb of a cell that can whip; the plural is *flagella*.

gizzard (GIH-zurd)—An organ found in the digestive system of earthworms and other animals, used to grind food.

hydrothermal (HY-droh-ther-mul) **vent**—An opening in the seafloor that expels hot gases.

invertebrate (in-VER-tuh-brit)—An animal without a backbone.

iridophore (ir-IH-duh-for)—A special color cell that reflects light.

larva (LAR-vuh)—The immature state of invertebrate animals; the plural is *larvae* (LAR-vee).

leucophore (LOO-kuh-for)—A special color cell that reflects light to look white.

lubricant (LOO-brih-kint)—A substance such as grease that allows two solids to slide easily past each other.

mollusk (MOL-usk)—An invertebrate with a soft body that is often covered by a shell.

nudibranch (NOO-dih-bronk)—A marine mollusk that has no shell or true gills.

parasite (PAYR-uh-syt)—An organism that feeds off a host organism, which harms the host.

Porifera (por-IH-fuh-ruh)—The scientific classification for sponges; it means "pore bearer."

porosity (por-AH-sih-tee)—The property of being porous or being able to absorb liquids.

proboscis (proh-BOS-is)—Long, flexible snout.

radula (RAD-yoo-luh)—A tongue-like band of tissue that contains rows of small teeth; it is used for scraping off particles of food and bringing them into the mouth and for drilling into prey.

saturated (SAT-chuh-ray-ted)—Completely wet.

sessile (SEH-sil)—Permanently attached to something; not able to move around.

simple animal—An animal without a backbone, including worms, sponges, and mollusks.

suspension (sus-PEN-shun) **feeder**—An animal that feeds by straining materials from water.

symbiosis (sim-bee-OH-sis)—A relationship between two different organisms, in which both organisms benefit.

tentacle (TEN-tih-kul)—One of the long arms of an octopus, used for feeling, moving, and grasping.

toxin (TOK-sin)—Any kind of poison.

adaptation 16, 34
annelid 7
anterior 24, 26
bacteria 28
bioluminescent 22
camouflage 34
casting 4
cephalopod 38
chromatophore 34–35
clam 5, 6, 7, 38
clitellum 25, 26
compost 4, 37
cuttlefish 6, 34–35
decomposer 4
diffusion 12
earthworm 7, 8, 24, 25, 26, 27
Fibonacci 30–32
filter feeder 4, 10, 11
flagellum 10
gastropod 36
gizzard 4, 25
heart 24–27
hydrothermal vent 28
invertebrate 4, 14
iridophore 35
larva 8, 28
leech 8, 18–21
leucophore 35
lubricant 36
mantle 5

mollusk 4, 5, 6, 7, 8, 9, 31, 34, 36, 38
nudibranch 6
octopus 5, 38, 39, 41
Osborn, Karen 22
osculum 10
parasite 7, 8, 18
pore 5, 10, 14, 15
Porifera 5
porosity 14, 15
proboscis 18
radula 7, 38
science notebook 9, 11, 19, 37
sessile 10, 16
shell 5–6, 16, 30, 31, 32, 36, 38
simple animal 4, 5, 7, 12, 16
siphon 38
slug 9
snail 4, 5, 6, 7, 31, 36, 37
sponge 4, 5, 8, 9, 10, 11, 12, 13, 14, 15, 16, 17, 34
symbiosis 16, 28
tentacle 29
tissues 4
toxin 5
tubeworm 4, 28–29
vermicomposting 4
worm 4, 7, 8, 9, 17, 18, 19, 20, 21, 22, 24–27, 28, 29

ABOUT THE AUTHOR

Colleen Kessler is the author of science books for kids, including *A Project Guide to the Solar System* and *A Project Guide to Reptiles and Birds* for Mitchell Lane Publishers. A former teacher of gifted students, Colleen now satisfies her curiosity as a full-time nonfiction writer. She does research and writes in her home office overlooking a wooded backyard in Northeastern Ohio. You can often find her blasting off rockets or searching for salamanders with her husband, Brian, and kids, Trevor, Molly, and Logan, or talking to schoolchildren about the excitement of studying science and nature. For more information about her books and presentations, or to invite her for a school visit, browse her website at http://www.colleen-kessler.com.